***IMPORTAN

Dear Customer,

Here is your copy of **‘Maui Catches The Sun’** by Janet Grierson. We trust it will provide you with everything you need to put on a memorable production.

Please read carefully the **Performance Licence Application** details on page 2 of this booklet. For any performance of drama, narrative and dialogue from published materials like this you are legally required to purchase a valid performance licence **from the publishers** – in this case Edgy Productions. This is standard practice. Please note that **local authority issued licences, PRS and CCLI licences do not cover these performances.**

If it is your intention to only use this material within the classroom as a learning activity, or to just sing the songs only in assemblies (using overhead transparencies) and not to an audience of parents, no fee is due.* In these circumstances you are covered by those licences mentioned above. **If, however you intend to make photocopies for any of these purposes, a fee is payable.**

Please complete the form on page 2 and post your performance details (with fee if applicable) no later than 28 days before your first performance, and a licence will be issued.

Should you have any questions regarding this matter, or the staging of ‘Maui Catches The Sun’ please get in touch and we will be happy to help in any way we can.

* Where no fee is due you are still obliged to return a Performance Application form – see p2

**************** *IMPORTANT* ****************

PERFORMANCE LICENCE APPLICATION FORM

For *any* performance of **Maui Catches The Sun**, a valid performance licence from Edgy Productions *must* be held. Please note, *your PRS, MCPS or CCLI licence does not cover you for performances of this production*. Please ensure you complete and return the relevant sections of this form, along with the fee where applicable, at least 28 days before your first performance. You can also apply online at www.edgyproductions.com

For performances where an admission charge is made, a form will be sent which you should return with 10% of the takings (plus VAT @ 17.5%) within 28 days of the final performance.

By ticking please indicate which performance licence applies to you, and send a photocopy of this form along with the fee (where applicable) to:

Permissions, Edgy Productions, 4 Queen Street, Uppingham, Rutland LE159QR

A copy of your Performance Licence will be posted to you

Licence 1	Licence 2	Licence 3
For up to 5 performances in one year, of only the songs, within school, to only staff and children of that school, at which no admission is charged, and for which no rehearsal photocopies are made:	*For up to 5 performances in one year, of the script and/or songs, to the public/parents, at which no admission is charged:*	*For up to 5 performances in one year, of the script and/or songs, to the public/parents, at which an admission charge is made:*
NO FEE ☐	**£25** *(inc VAT)* ☐	**£25** *(inc VAT)* + 10% of takings *(plus VAT @ 17.5%)* ☐
This licence allows only the use of handwritten transparencies of songs. No photocopies allowed	*This licence includes permission to photocopy the script and songs*	*This licence includes permission to photocopy the script and songs*

Writers rely on payments from public performances for their livelihoods. Please ensure they receive their dues.

NAME............................**SCHOOL**...

ADDRESS ....

TEL.......................... **EMAIL**...

Number of performances......... **Dates of performances from** .... **to** ....

I enclose a cheque for £25 *(if applicable)* **payable to Edgy Productions Ltd** ☐
Please send me an invoice for £25 *(if applicable)* **to be paid within 30 days** ☐ Tick one box

YOU CAN NOT RECORD YOUR PERFORMANCE/S AND SELL OR GIVE AWAY VIDEO, DVD, CD OR CASSETTE DUPLICATIONS, WITHOUT PURCHASING A FURTHER LICENCE FROM EDGY PRODUCTIONS. PLEASE CONTACT US FOR DETAILS. SHOULD YOU MAKE AND DISTRIBUTE RECORDINGS WITHOUT THIS LICENCE YOU WILL BE IN BREACH OF COPYRIGHT LAW.

INTRODUCTION

One of the most well-known Maori tales is beautifully brought to life through incredibly catchy songs and a witty script. This new musical, by established New Zealand writer Janet Grierson, tells of Maui's daring quest to bring more sunlight to the struggling people of Aotearoa. It is easily adaptable to suit a larger or smaller cast, and a wide range of children's ages and abilities. Whether you want to put on a full-blown musical performance or simply use it to enhance your studies of cultural history, 'Maui Catches The Sun' is a fantastic resource for your school.

=====

Opening with the song *'Too Short Were The Days'* we witness the hardship of the Maori villagers, who suffer short days and long nights because the sun races too quickly across the sky. The men have no time to complete their hunting and fishing expeditions, the women cannot see to prepare meals or to do their weaving, and the children do not have enough hours of daylight to enjoy their games and dancing. In the song *'Slow Down Sun'* they plead for more hours of sunlight.

Maui, who has performed many great deeds for the ancient people of Aotearoa, is asked by the village elders to help them in their plight. He summons his brothers who nervously agree to join him on a journey to the edge of the world, where they will *'Catch the sun'* (song).

Maui tells the women of the village that a snare will be needed with which to trap the sun, and they enthusiastically set about *'Weaving'* (song) flax to make strong ropes for this very purpose.

Maui and his brothers set out on their treacherous quest, and finally reach the pit from which the sun rises and begins its all-too-quick journey across the sky. With skill and daring they snare the sun and Maui beats it with his magic whale jawbone, demanding that it travels more slowly. The sun struggles but is no match for the hero. Battered and defeated it promises to do as it is asked, if only the men *'Release The Ropes'* (song).

Triumphantly, Maui and his brothers return to find the people enjoying their longer, sunnier days. With a reprise of the song *'Too Short Were The Days'* they celebrate their freedom to fish, hunt, cook, weave and play, and joyfully thank Maui for coming to their rescue.

CHARACTERS
Speaking parts in order of appearance

Narrator

Children 1 and 2

Women 1, 2, 3, 4 and 5

Children 3 and 4

Man 1

Village Elder

Man 2

villagers

Maui

Taha

Roto

Waho

Pae

brothers

The Sun

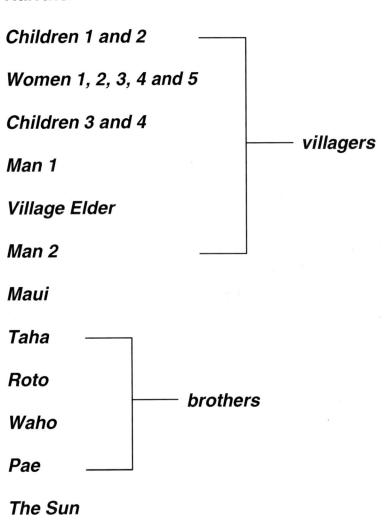

Ensemble Characters – for a larger cast

More men

More women

More children

Choir

<u>Scene 1</u>

*(To **intro music (cd track 7)** the cast enters. Groups of men, women and children are seen working, cooking, weaving, practising poi dances and stick games etc – see staging suggestions. A narrator stands to the side holding an old looking manuscript from which s/he will read.)*

Song – <u>Too Short Were The days</u> *(cd track 8)*
(Whole cast)

Verse 1   Listen to our story told from ages past,
Of how the sun moved across the sky too fast.
The people were unhappy and frustrated too,
They could not finish what they had begun to do.

Chorus   Too short were the days, too long were the nights.
Too few were the hours of daylight.
The sun moved too fast across the sky,
Too quickly the daylight hours passed by.

Verse 2   Maui was a hero so the legends told,
For he had great powers, he was strong and bold.
He thought upon a plan to make the sun go slow,
And so we have our story told from long ago.

Chorus   Too short were the days..........

Repeat   Too short were the days..........

Narrator ~ In the beginning of time in the land of Aotearoa, the sun travelled quickly across the sky. The days were too short and the nights were too long. There was very little time for the people to complete their tasks. The men needed more time to hunt and fish. The women wove flax mats and baskets and worked in the kumara gardens, but they could never finish their work. The children liked to dance, practise stick games and play, but it quickly became too dark for them to see. When they had prepared their meals, the sun would go down and they would have to eat in darkness. The people became unhappy and they grumbled about the days being too short.

*(To **intro music (cd track 9)** the working, poi dancing, stick games etc continue. Gradually dim the lights and fade the music. Sticks are dropped, pois are tangled and work ceases to the frustration of all.)*

Child 1 ~ *(practising stick games)* Oh, it's happened again! The sun's gone down and we can't see what we're doing!

Child 2 ~ I keep dropping my sticks! We can't practise in the dark!

Children ~ *(grizzling)* There's never any time to play.

Woman 1 ~ *(weaving)* It's always the same. Rush, rush, rush to get anything done before the sun goes down!

Woman 2 ~ *(weaving)* We can't keep up with our work. I'm only half way through weaving this mat. *(holding up unfinished mat)* and now I can't see to finish it. I keep making mistakes!

Woman 1 ~ Last week I was in the bush collecting berries in my flax basket. Before I knew it, the sun went down and I couldn't see to find my way back home. I tripped over tree roots, dropped the basket and lost all the berries.

(Everyone complains together with comments like 'The sun goes too fast!')

Woman 3 ~ We'll have to eat in darkness again!

Woman 4 ~ That's right. We can't even see our food!

Woman 3 ~ We can't see what we're eating and we can't see who we're eating with! Just last night, I sat down to eat with my husband, but it wasn't my husband at all! It was the wrong man!

(The women laugh at her.)

Woman 5 ~ That's because it was my husband!

Woman 3 ~ I hate having to eat in the dark.

Child 3 ~ *(to friend)* At least I can leave my vegetables and my mum won't know!

Child 4 ~ And I can sneak some extra meat off my dad's plate.

Woman 3 ~ *(standing up, moving off stage)* Come on everyone. Let's go.

*(To **intro music (cd track 10)** bring the lights down to signal the end of the day. Fade the music and bring the lights back up to signal a new day.)*

Man 1 ~ What can we do? Something must be done to make our days longer. We cannot live like this.

(The villagers shrug shoulders, shake their heads and look towards sky.)

Song – <u>Slow Down Sun</u> *(cd track 11)*
(Whole cast)

Chorus
(All)

Slow down sun, slow down sun,
We cannot get our work done.
Too quickly the days go past,
The hours of daylight do not last.

Verse 1
(Men)

There is no time for working, no time for hunting too.
There is no time for fishing, when we're out in our canoe.

Chorus Slow down sun……….

Verse 2
(Women)

There is no time for weaving, no time for gardening too.
There is no time for cooking, hours of daylight are too few.

Chorus Slow down sun……….

Verse 3
(Children)

There is no time for dancing, no time for playing too.
There is no time for doing all the things we like to do.

Chorus Slow down sun……….

Village Elder ~ *(stepping forward and speaking with authority)* Perhaps Maui can help us. Where is he?

Man 2 ~ He's in the forest hunting. I'll go and find him. *(He exits.)*

Village Elder ~ *(slowly and thoughtfully)* If anyone can come up with an idea, Maui can. He has achieved many great things that have seemed impossible.

(Maui enters, carrying hunting gear, amongst which is his enchanted whale jawbone.)

Village Elder ~ *(calling Maui over to him)* Ah, Maui. Can you help us? You have been blessed with great wisdom and special powers. What can we do to lengthen our days? They are too short and the nights are too long. It's so frustrating for all of us.

Maui ~ You are right. It's frustrating for me too. Just last night I was out fishing in the canoe. I had a big bite, I started to haul it in and it was a whopper! *(He shows exaggerated size with arm movements.)* I was just taking it off the hook when the sun went down. The fish slipped out of my hands and got away! I had to paddle the canoe back to land and drag it onto the beach in darkness. *(looking up to the sky and shaking his fist)* Something must be done! The sun races across the sky far too quickly. *(pausing)* With my magic jawbone and with your help, I think we can succeed in making the days longer.

(He beckons to his brothers and they stand together in a huddle as Maui explains his plan.)

Narrator ~ Maui called his brothers together and told them of his plan. They would travel to the edge of the world to catch the sun in a snare made from flax ropes.

Taha ~ *(stepping back in horror)* Catch the sun? Maui, you've come up with some good ideas before, but catching the sun? The heat and flames will burn us!

Roto ~ It's way too dangerous. The ropes will burn. They'll shrivel up in the heat.

Waho ~ You mean we'll shrivel up in the heat!

Pae ~ No one can get near the sun. It's impossible. He is far too hot and fierce.

Waho ~ Besides, I don't want to singe my hair.

Maui ~ Haven't you seen the things I have done already? I know we can do this but I can't do it alone. I need your help. *(turning to the women)* And I'll need your help too. We will need some long and strong ropes woven with flax so that we can make a snare.

(Maui and his brothers exit.)

Narrator ~ The women of the village gathered the flax from the nearby bushes. They worked hard day in and day out, skilfully weaving the long ropes.

Song – **Weaving** *(cd track 12)*
(The Women)

Verse 1   Over, under, round and through,
We will weave the flax for you.
Twisting, turning all day long,
Making ropes so very strong.

Verse 2   Over, under, round and through,
We will weave the flax for you.
Twisting, turning made with care,
Making ropes into a snare.

Verse 3   Over, under, round and through,
We will weave the flax for you.
Twisting, turning everyone,
Making ropes to catch the sun.

(Maui and brothers enter as the women finish their song. The women pass the ropes over to Maui.)

Maui ~ *(looking with admiration)* Ah, you have worked hard at this. *(holding them up)* These are thick, strong ropes. They will be good.

Woman 1 ~ Here. We have prepared some food and water for you. You'll need it for the long journey ahead.

(She passes over flax baskets and jars of water.)

Maui ~ *(turning to his brothers)* Look at you Waho, with your strong back, broad shoulders and muscular arms. *(Waho boastfully flexes his muscles.)* Just look at those muscles. Here, you can carry the ropes.

(Maui places the ropes over his shoulders as he groans and stoops under the weight. The other brothers laugh at him.)

Look at you Taha with your skinny arms and your fat free body. You need fattening up. You can carry the food. *(The other brothers laugh at him.)* Roto and Pae, you can take the jars of water.

(All the brothers struggle under the weight they are carrying.)

Brothers ~ What are you taking Maui?

Maui ~ Me? Well, I'm taking you, my brothers.

Song – <u>Catch The Sun</u> *(cd track 13)*
(Maui and the bothers)

Verse 1   To the edge of the world, over mountains high,
We will travel to where the sun will rise.
Crossing through streams over valleys low,
To the edge of the world we will go.

Chorus   And we will catch the sun, catch the sun,
We will catch the sun if we can.
Catch the sun, catch the sun, to catch the sun is the plan.

Verse 2   To the edge of the world, past the kauri tree,
We will travel to where the sun will be.
Through native bush where the pungas grow,
To the edge of the world we will go.

Chorus   And we will catch the sun..........

Verse 3   To the edge of the world through the forests green,
We will travel to where we have never been.
Travelling at night so the sun won't know,
To the edge of the world we will go.

               And we will catch the sun..........

Maui ~ Walk quickly brothers, while there is darkness.

*(To **intro music (cd track 14)** bring the lights down. Maui and brothers exit.)*

Narrator ~ Maui, with his enchanted weapon, led his brothers on their long journey. They set off in the direction of the rising sun. Carrying the flax ropes over their shoulders, they travelled secretly at night while the sun slept.

(Maui and the brothers enter. The lights are still dimmed.)

Pae ~ *(wearily)* Ah, how much further Maui? I need to stop and rest.

Maui ~ Not much longer now. It's just over the mountain, through the stream, along the bush track, past the kauri forest, over the swamp, down the cliff, around the bog, along the coast *(triumphantly)* and then we'll be at the edge of the world.

Pae ~ So we're nearly there?

Maui ~ That's right bro. Come on.

*(They exit. To **intro music (cd track 15)** the stage is made ready for the next scene – see staging suggestions. Fade the music when ready. Maui and the brothers enter. The lights are still dimmed.)*

Scene 2

Narrator ~ During the day, they lay down in the long grass and slept behind rocks. At night they continued their journey until at last they came to the edge of the world. Spreading the snare across the sky, they waited in silence, ready to catch the sun when it rose. Patiently, they waited until dawn. Maui held his magic jawbone in one hand and the ropes of the snare in the other.

(The lights come up to the scene at the pit of the sun – see staging suggestions)

Suddenly, the ground trembled and shook. Like a burning fire, the sun began to emerge.

*(To the **Sunrise** sound effect **(cd track 16)** the sun appears and is snared by Maui and the brothers. The lights flash and the **Struggle Music (cd track 17)** begins. The following dialogue is spoken loudly, and in some instances shouted, over the music.)*

Maui muttered a charm and sprang to his feet. His brothers leaped from their hiding places. Pulling tightly on their ropes, they snared the sun and held him captive.

Maui ~ Pull the ropes! Quickly, pull the ropes! Hold him brothers while I beat him with my magic jawbone.

Sun ~ *(screaming)* What's this? What are you doing? Let me go!

Maui ~ Keep pulling tightly!

Sun ~ Aie-e-e! Let me go! Let me go! You are hurting me!

Maui ~ Hold on brothers! He's starting to lose his strength!

Sun ~ What do you want from me?

Pae ~ Don't kill him Maui. We still need him for light and warmth.

Taha ~ *(shielding his eyes and holding on to the rope with only one hand)* He's blinding my eyes.

Maui ~ Keep pulling just a bit longer! He's weakening.

Narrator ~ The brothers pulled the ropes harder and harder as Maui beat the sun fiercely with his magic weapon. Straining, struggling and screaming with pain, the sun pleaded for his life.

Sun ~ Stop it! Let me go! Why are you hitting me? *(Fade the Struggle Music.)*

Song – <u>Release The Ropes</u> *(cd track 18)*
(The Sun supported by whole cast)

Verse 1
(Sun)

Release the ropes and let me go,
I promise you that I will go slow.
Let go the ropes, stop hitting me,
I ask you Maui, set me free.
Just let me go.

Verse 2
(Sun)

Release the ropes and let me go,
I promise you that I will go slow.
Let go the ropes, I'll share with you
My heat and light the whole day through.
Just let me go.

Middle 8
(All)

Let him go, let him go,
He has promised that he will go slow.
Let him go, let him go,
He has promised to go slow.

Verse 3
(Sun)

Release the ropes and let me go,
I promise you that I will go slow.
Let go the ropes, I'll send my rays
To shine more hours throughout the days
Just let me go.
Just let me go.

Maui ~ Listen to me. I'll let you go if you promise to slow down and give us more hours in the day. You move too quickly across the sky. We don't have enough time to complete our tasks. You must promise to slow down. Do you promise?

Sun ~ I promise, I promise! Please let me go. I couldn't go quickly now even if I tried. *(slowly and weakly)* You have wounded me so badly. You have taken all my strength.

Narrator ~ When the sun was weak and tired, Maui gave the signal and the brothers released the ropes that held him captive.

*(To **intro music (cd track 19)** the lights fade and all exit. The stage is made ready for the next scene, the Maori village. When ready, bring the lights up and fade the music.)*

<u>Scene 3</u>
(The women are sitting in groups laughing as they weave, the children are playing stick games and practising poi dances, and the men are carrying hunting weapons.)

Narrator ~ From then on, the sun kept his promise and moved slowly across the sky. When Maui and his brothers returned home to their village, they found the women laughing and talking as they worked long into the evening. The men were able to hunt, fish and carve and the children danced and played with great jubilation.

(Maui and the brothers enter.)

Village Elder ~ Maui! Our hero! Welcome home.

(The elder greets Maui with a 'hongi' - a Maori greeting of respect in which the noses are gently pressed together.)

Men ~ *(calling out comments like…)* Welcome home! We have so much more time now! etc.

Women ~ *(calling out comments like…)* The days are so much longer. We have plenty of time now to do all the things we want to do.

Children ~ *(calling out comments like…)* We've got much more time to play! And to eat! Thank you Maui!

3rd country dance group.

(At this point you can include any extra Maori songs and dances you may have learned, as part of the celebrations.)

Boat song

Narrator ~ The people of the village celebrated the return of Maui and his brothers with much feasting, singing and dancing. Everyone was happy, for now they had time to do all the things they wanted to.

Song – <u>Too Short Were The days - Reprise</u> *(cd track 20)*
(Whole cast)

Verse 1 That has been our story told from ages past
(All)   Of how the sun moved across the sky too fast
     We are now so happy and delighted too for
     We can finish anything that we want to.

P.+N

Chorus Now long are the days and short are the nights
(All)   We have more hours of daylight.
     We thank you Maui for what you have done
     You lengthened our days by slowing the sun.

Repeat Now long are the days……….
(All)

The End

STAGING SUGGESTIONS

Firstly, if you need ideas for the overall look of your production, or would like more information about Maori culture in general to help with any aspect of the show's content, the following websites are recommended;

www.waitahaculturalcouncil.co.nz/teams.html

www.experiencenz.com/gallerymc.cfm *good photos.*

www. nzti.com/mitai/index.htm

We suggest a staging layout similar to this, which will allow the entire cast to be on view all the time, and to be heard during all the songs. Actors and groups seated to the side will be able to move easily into and out of prominent positions for their featured songs, dialogue or choreography. For the entrance and exit of individual characters, space can be made behind display boards either side of the main stage, or a 'channel' can be created through the audience.

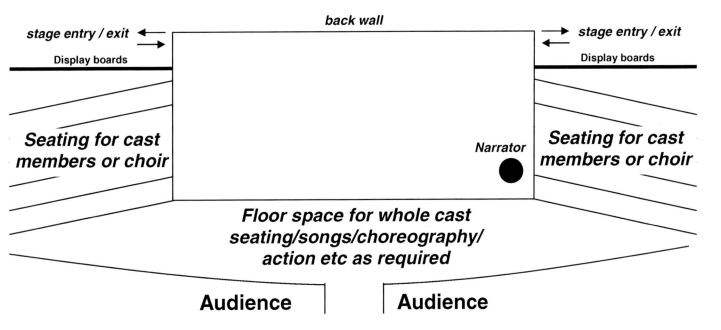

back wall

stage entry / exit Display boards

stage entry / exit Display boards

Seating for cast members or choir

Seating for cast members or choir

Narrator

Floor space for whole cast seating/songs/choreography/ action etc as required

Audience **Audience**

Scenery – There are two scenes which need to be represented in the story. Firstly there is the village, for which you could create a backdrop depicting a Maori meeting house set amongst native bush. For the second scene you will need to represent the sun's pit. If possible change the backdrop to one showing a desolate and rocky landscape, and make large boulders to set around the stage. If it is too difficult to change backdrops for the second scene then perhaps pin grey or neutral-coloured material in front of the village backdrop, and remove it for the final scene.

Costumes – These are some simple ideas that can be used for costuming, however more authentic costume ideas can be found on the suggested websites. <u>Maori men and boys</u> should be bare footed, and could wear black shorts with flax skirts made from brown paper. Alternatively they can be bare-chested. Tikis (ornamental necklaces) can be worn around their necks. Some of the Maori men, particularly the Maori Elder and Maui, could have facial tattoos applied with face paints. Again, look at the websites for ideas. Women and girls should also be bare-footed, and could wear black strap tops and flax skirts (made from brown paper). In addition they could wear head bands coloured red, black and white with Maori motifs, and also tikis around their necks. Some of the women might have a moko (a tattoo) on their chin. The sun's costume could comprise a full yellow cape from the neck to the ground, with a large yellow cardboard circle behind the actor's head.

Props – You will need:
- Sticks for stick games. Maori stick games are rhythm games played by two or more people sitting opposite each other, cross-legged. They perform various patterns of stick actions to the beat. These may include tapping to the side or together and throwing and catching from person to person.
- Pois. A poi is a soft ball attached to a cord. It can be short (about 30cm) or long (about 60 cm). They are gracefully swung by women dancers in action songs.
- Knucklebones (like jacks) or spinning tops for the children.
- Flax baskets, flax mats, flax ropes and cooking pots for the women.
- Fishing traps, clubs and paddles made from card, for the men.
- A decorative bone carving for Maui's magic jawbone. In the absence of a real bone you could make one from card or perhaps papier maché.
- Two long ropes will be needed for the 'catching' of the sun. Alternatively the sun's costume could have ropes already attached, the ends of which the brothers pick up and pull from either side. Maui would stand centrally to beat the sun.

Use of Space – The whole cast will probably want to be involved in the performance of most, if not all, of the songs. A space on the floor in front of the main stage could be used to accommodate extra bodies. In this space, for some songs, the cast could perform dance routines or act out the lyrical content. A seating area for resting performers to one side of the stage lets them enjoy the performance as part of the audience, allows easy movement on and off the stage, and of course eliminates the need for back-stage supervision.

Audience seating – Finally, we suggest the audience be seated at tables (cabaret style), and encouraged to bring drinks and nibbles of their choice. A relaxed party atmosphere will really make the evening go with a swing, and give parents, staff and children something to remember for a long time. Please email, phone or write to us if you have any production queries at all, and we'll be more than happy to help.

1. Too Short Were The Days

Words and music by Janet Grierson

1.Lis - ten to our sto - ry told from a - ges__ past, of
2.Mau - i was the he - ro so the leg - ends told,

how the sun moved a-cross the sky too__ fast the peo - ple were un-hap-py and frus
he had great pow-ers he was strong and bold. He thought up - on a plan to make the

tra - ted__ too,__ they could not fin - ish what they had be - gun to do
sun go__ slow, and so we have our sto - ry told from long a - go.

2. Slow Down Sun

Words and music by Janet Grierson

3. Weaving

Words and music by Janet Grierson

1. O - ver,__ un - der, ro - und and through, we w - ill weave the flax for you. Twist - ing, turn-ing all day long, mak - ing ropes so ve - ry strong.
2. O - ver,__ un - der, ro - und and through, we w - ill weave the flax for you. Twist - ing, turn-ing made with care, mak - ing ropes in - to a snare.
3. O - ver,__ un - der, ro - und and through, we w - ill weave the flax for you. Twist - ing, turn-ing ev' - ry - one, mak - ing ropes to catch the sun.

4. Catch The Sun

Words and music by Janet Grierson

5. Release The Ropes

Words and music by Janet Grierson

Bridge. Let him go,— let him go.—

He has pro-mised that he will go slow. Let him go,—

let him go,— he has pro-mised to go slow.

3.Re lease the ropes a-nd let me go,— I

pro - mise you that I will go_ slow. Let go the ropes I'll send my rays

to shine more hours_ through - out the days. Just let me go.

Just let me go.

6. Too Short Were The Days - Reprise

Words and music by Janet Grierson

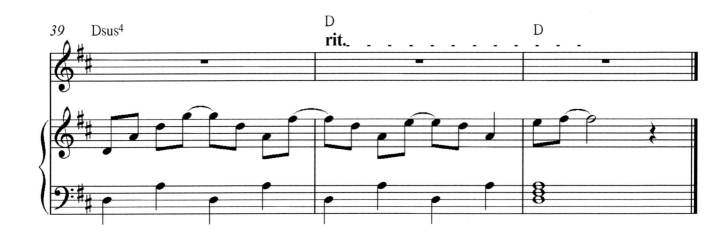